Making Sense
An Elder's Task

Gerry Tamm

For Jerry with a J, who keeps me laughing.

Contents

Preface

Stories have to be told or they die, and when they die,
we can't remember who we are or why we're here.
Sue Monk Kidd

Everyone has a story to tell. By listening to each other's stories, we learn about the world. This has been true from the earliest days when we gathered around the evening fire in caves, to the troubadours, to sewing circles, AA meetings, and TED talks on the internet. Our stories shape us. As we age we piece together our own stories. This is how we make sense of our lives.

These are my stories.

Wisdom Panel Speech
Delivered at Gather the Elders
Tucson, Arizona, January 10, 2012

When I was a little girl in Sunday School, I heard the story of Solomon. Offered the choice of power, wealth, or wisdom, he chose wisdom and got it all. I thought that was pretty smart and decided I wanted wisdom too. Well here I am on a wisdom panel. It took me 80 years to get here and I have 8 minutes to tell you about it. But I'm only going to talk about the last ten. That's when I met Del and found out about Elder Circles.

At that time my husband and I had sold our family home and bought a small house in Tucson and a condo in Michigan. When we retired we became official snowbirds and enjoyed the best of all worlds. The mountains and desert in the winter, the lakes in summer. We danced two or three times a week–square dancing and round dancing. We traveled. We explored Arizona. We discovered OASIS [an educational, social organization for older adults] where I took classes and taught. We made new friends. Life was good.

Then our knees started to complain. We had to sell our beloved three level condo in the heart of Dearborn when the stairs became too much, especially when we were lugging groceries. We moved into a small apartment on the 11th floor of a senior high rise. Next we had to give up dancing while we waited for, and recovered from, knee replacements. Three so far, one more in May. Thank goodness we only have two knees each and that there are replacement parts. Our activities were limited to the amount of walking involved. No more concerts at the University or science lectures. We couldn't walk from the parking lot to the auditorium. We were losing friends. Our physical activities slowed down.

It was time to get our spiritual lives in order and that's where Elder Circles came in. I attended my first Circle at OASIS. Del was the facilitator. Our first exercise was to review our lives. We divided our lives into ten year segments and looked at who we were, what we were doing, and what we learned during each period. It was the first step in harvesting our lives. Time to celebrate our accomplishments, let go of our regrets–we call that life repair–and discover our purpose. I found my fellow travelers on the Wisdom Journey and attended regularly. Life was good.

After a few years, life was comfortable but something was missing. I felt purposeless. I needed more. Now I have to backtrack a bit.

When we moved into our apartment in Dearborn, I hated it. The apartment was lovely really. The glass wall of our living room looked out over a sea of treetops and local landmarks with the Detroit skyline in the distance. One of our neighbors said it looked like Central Park. But the atmosphere in the building was stultifying. There was no welcoming committee. People greeted us in the halls and elevator but that was about it.

So at Christmas we held an open house in our apartment for the 11th floor residents. Everyone came, enjoyed themselves, then retreated to their closed doors. The doors had automatic closers on them so you had to fight to get in and out of your apartment. We took ours off. We even left our door open one Sunday. People gawked and said "Nobody's ever done that before." They said that after the open house too. We thought it was the motto of the building: "Nobody's ever done that before."

Well we went off to Arizona and when we returned that spring, the atmosphere was toxic. People were angry. No smiles. We found out that our tyrannical building manager and equally tyrannical board president had fired Tom our friendly, trustworthy, dependable, helpful maintenance man and hired an impersonal cleaning service in his place. People were not happy.

So we got together with two other couples on the 11th floor and decided to do something about it. We recruited five people and talked them into running for the board with the express purpose of getting Tom back. We called them the Fab Five and vigorously campaigned for them.

They were elected and their first act was to rehire Tom. The building manager walked out in a huff and the board set about working on the neglected infrastructure of the 30- year- old building and putting the finances in order. The new president had been a facilities manager at Chrysler and the treasurer was an accountant. They hired a management company. We were in good hands and life settled down to the normal routine. Doors of the apartments closed again.

That brings us back to my purposelessness. It occurred to me that what Morley needed was an Elder Circle. So I found a partner to work with who would take over while I was gone and we called our first Circle in May two years ago. We had 16 people that day and we started out with the life review. Instead of the ten segments we divided our lives into spring, summer, fall, and winter. People loved it. In their small groups they found out things about each other they had never known even though they had lived together for years. They were excited.

We have met monthly ever since. There are usually about twelve people–not always the same ones–three of them were men. We've lost a few and gained a few. We are a new Morley tradition. And I have found my purpose.

It is to pass on what I can–we call that mentoring–and I will continue to pass it on until I pass on.

The Veil

Earth's crammed with heaven . . .
Elizabeth Barrett Browning

Behind the Veil

After the beginning
Vibration and Form, the two elementary principles,
individuated and divided
(Yet we always find them intertwined.)
Sumerian creation song, circa 2000 BCE

We live in a parallel universe. The mystics know this. The poets know this. The prophets know this. And the scientists know this. They call it the multiverse and they have posited string theory to explain it..

How do I know it? Perhaps it is from watching *Star Trek*. But then why am I attracted to that and not to Freddie Krueger? Perhaps it is because of psychotherapy which opened the world of dreams to me. Perhaps it is the lectures on mystics by a medievalist professor, or by a Buddhist at the Episcopal church, or a Kabbalist at the Jewish temple. I'm sure of it from reading poets and from visiting Ireland and from the Bible. It is from my own experience.

I think that all of these thinkers are describing the same thing in the language that is available to them. Mystics tell us that their visions cannot be described in words and they use images. Poets use metaphors. Prophets claim revelations from God. Scientists have their own language, usually mathematics, often unintelligible to the average person. They make up words for new discoveries like "quarks" and "bosons." So from the cacophony of often conflicting voices, I have come to my own conclusions and have chosen voices that support my view.

When Steve Jobs died, his last words were "Oh wow! Oh wow! Oh wow!" (I put in the exclamation points.) What did he see? This man who saw the possibilities of the computer, who understood the vibrations in the universe that made those possibilities reality, who changed the world, saw something. I think it was what awaits all of us. I think he saw heaven, but the heaven he saw was probably not the pearly gates described by John in *Revelation*. I think it was the parallel universe that surrounds us but that we are unable to see because of the limitations of our bodies. The best analogy I have for this comes from the physicist Dr. Michio Kaku, the TV guru of science and a founder of string theory. He explained that all the radio waves from stations all over the world are available in any single room, but we can only hear the one that our radio is tuned in to.

It is easy to say that Ireland is a land of superstition. Who has ever seen a leprechaun or found a pot of gold or even the end of a rainbow? It is also a home of the Druids, whose spiritual beliefs in nature are alive and well today and whose knowledge of astronomy still astounds us. And of the monks who preserved the literature of the world as they copied great works in their monasteries during the dark ages when libraries were destroyed. The Irish treasure their sacred sites, the thin places where the veil between the reality we know and the eternal world is lifted. Tourists who visit these stone structures report a feeling of energy and lifting of the spirits. Sedona, Arizona has its own version of these places called vortexes which draw thousands of visitors each year to experience the spiritual lift. They anger the Indians by moving sacred stones into circles.

All of this is brushed off by skeptics as New Age nonsense. But think of the physicists who discovered quantum mechanics in the nineteen fifties and have made amazing inroads to this unknown reality which the ancients have known from the very beginning.

The ancients understood that the first act of creation was the separation of vibration and form which they called heaven and earth. Scientists today call this wave and particle. The big bang theory–confirmed most recently by the Hadron super collider–describes this separation. These two principles are always intertwined and can only be understood by looking at the properties of one or the other at any given time. It is the basis of today's scientific study. It is the basis of my belief that we are present in a universe beyond our perception. Religions call this the omnipresence of God. Physicists call it the Higgs field. Alcoholics Anonymous calls it the Higher Power. Obe-Wan Kenobi called it the force. It is at the very least a sense of wonder at something larger than ourselves that cosmology and psychology tell us is within ourselves. We are all made of stardust.

There's Something About the Desert

What makes the desert beautiful is that
somewhere it hides a well.
Antoine de Saint-Exupery

"Looks like scrub to me," Sally said as we drove through the desert. *My beautiful desert? How could she?* I said nothing.

When folks come to visit us in Tucson for the first time, we take them to Red Hills, the visitors center in Saguaro National Park West. They show a gorgeous slide show of desert scenes with a commentary by a Tohono O'odham Indian. The ending is spectacular. We love to hear the audience gasp when the curtains slowly open to reveal a panoramic view of the actual desert. The Tohono O'odham–desert people–have great respect for their home and reverence for its beauty. I never tire of seeing that film and listening to the soothing voice of the narrator.

I fell in love with the desert the first time I saw it. There is a mystery to it. I thought that nothing grew there. I was wrong. The soil looks barren but it is alive with growth. When we first saw our new house, there was nothing in the back yard and the soil looked hopeless. We returned a month later to find two giant tumbleweeds rolling around. We covered the ground with rocks, common landscaping in Tucson, and planted cactus and agaves and a three foot high palo verde.

Fifteen years later that tree was higher than the house and it requires severe pruning every year to keep it away from the roof. We have a desert garden of fairy duster, Mexican honeysuckle, feathery cassia, Texas ranger, and Mexican bird of paradise, all shrubs that require very little water and can survive the desert heat and the occasional night freezes.

But it is not just the garden that grows so profusely. It is my own creativity. It reminds me of Mary Shelley's comment: "Invention does not consist in creating out of void, but out of chaos." It is the peaceful voice of that Tohono O'odham in the film and the silence of the desert. It is the surprise of cactus flowers and the ocotillo torches after the occasional rains, the ever-shifting mountains as the backdrop for this beauty. My inner chaos finds respite here and I bloom.

And so it is the desert that puts me in touch with myself. Sometimes this is a strange experience. One night we were driving through the desert on the way to a bonfire meeting with Johnny and Susan. In the course of our conversation Johnny mentioned a writer who wrote about Africa but he couldn't recall his name. "Robert Ruark," I said. I don't know why I remembered that name. He had written *Something of Value,* a novel about Africa which I vaguely recall reading. The novel was published in 1955 and it was the only work of his I have ever read, but his name popped into my head out of nowhere some fifty years later.

On another drive through the desert, same circumstances, another name popped up. This time it was the answer to a question that had been bothering me for a couple of years. What was the name of that park in Detroit where my grade school class had picnicked on more than one occasion? I had googled. I had asked friends. I had even driven through the area where I thought it was. Nothing. Then, in a barren, unparklike desert, two thousand miles away, I suddenly knew. It was Lola Valley.

I am astonished by what is stored in my brain. Or perhaps in a parallel universe, in something like the cloud filled with data that businesses access by computers when needed. When I ask a question, the answer will come to me, sometimes at the most unexpected times and in the most unexpected places.

Signs

---

*. . . you must follow the signs. God inscribed on the world
the path that each man must follow. It is just a matter of
reading the inscription he wrote for you.*
Paulo Coelho

Road Signs

Two roads diverged in a wood, and I—
I took the one less traveled by. . .
                    Robert Frost

There are no signs on the road to Hell. I discovered this on a beautiful autumn Saturday when I took a cross country drive across Michigan to the fall convention of the Michigan Poetry Society at Olivet College.

I spent the night before the meeting at our cottage in Hell, a townlet–really a crossroads–in Michigan. I checked the map and discovered that Olivet was directly west of us about halfway between two expressways, as was Hell. But there was a county road that ran across the state between Hell and Olivet. Why not?

Now the thing about county roads is that they often turn on to the local roads of small towns and change street names in the process. This was no problem for me as I set out and drove through farmlands with little traffic and lovely scenery. At each turn there was a sign pointing the way to Bellevue, the town after Olivet. I followed the signs without paying much attention to the various turns or street names.

After an inspiring day with my fellow poets, I set off

for Hell. By then the sun had given way to clouds. This was important because I no longer had the sun to indicate my direction and my car had no compass. Getting out of Olivet was no problem. But the first town I came to had two roads leading out of town and no sign to indicate which one I should take. After trying both and not recognizing the surroundings of either one–had I passed that park on the way to Olivet?–I retraced my route back to a gas station on the road I came in on. Following directions I got out of that town and was on my way again.

I knew Stockbridge so I was on the right route. Then I found Doyle, a road that would take me home to Hell. Well, it didn't. Obviously this Doyle was not the road I knew. I ended up in a community of homes and farms, and I lost my way with all the twists and turns. I struggled to find my way out without the benefit of a compass so that when I came to another major road, I didn't know whether I was north or south of it.

By then it was dark. I soon realized I had turned the wrong way. When I finally saw a sign to Gregory, I took it. It was the long way home but at least I knew where I was. Eventually I found my way and pulled into our yard with great relief. Hell is not as easy to get to as some people think regardless of your intentions.

And so we rely on signs not only to get around geographically but also to make our way through life. The signs are there but we sometimes don't recognize them and they are not the same for everyone. Paulo Coelho defines them as our alphabet for communication with God. I think of them as guideposts that tell me I am on the right path.

God Has a Sense of Humor

If you could choose one characteristic that would get you through life, choose a sense of humor.
Jennifer Jones

One perfect Michigan spring morning, after breakfast with friends at a local family restaurant, I was driving home feeling on top of the world. I turned into the boulevard entrance to the parking lot of our apartment building. Thunk. The rear fender of my Sable took the blow of some monster SUV that suddenly backed into it.

I stopped the car, got out to survey the damage, and saw my neighbor's daughter ranting at someone who had apparently backed up suddenly causing her to back up reflexively into my car. I saw no need for a police report. Her mother was a friend. I said we'd let the insurance company sort it out. That turned out to be a mistake.

I called AAA and expected her to call her insurance company. She did not. When AAA finally reached her after several attempts, she told them she had not hit me and was not responsible for any damage to my car. The details of what followed are not important to this story. But after much mental anguish and the inconvenience of auto repair, dealing

13

with insurance companies, phone calls and letters, my claim was denied and we were out the $550.00 deductible.

Not about to give in, I decided to go to Small Claims Court and began to prepare my case. I gathered my documents and filled in all the necessary forms. But as they say, pictures are worth a thousand words and so I decided to take pictures of the scene. One day when we were driving into the parking lot, I asked my husband to stay in the car at the entrance while I got out to take pictures that would show the relative position of cars in the area. A car was pulling in just then and I caught the perfect snapshot to make my case. Surprise. It was my neighbor driving in! The mother of the perpetrator.

My husband and I giggled as we rode the elevator up to our apartment. This was a good sign. We felt like a couple of kids caught in the act of something we weren't supposed to be doing.

Sadly the girl lied in court but the facts, backed up with the photos I had arranged with my computer, clearly supported my claim, and the magistrate ruled in my favor. Unsatisfied with that verdict, she appealed to a judge, which required a repeat performance. The judge listened to the story, examined the evidence–the pictures again–then asked her one simple question: "Why did you get out of your car?"

I don't remember her answer, if she had one, but the verdict was again in my favor. It took a few more phone calls to get the check out of her insurance company but we persevered and so eventually had the last laugh.

The House I Live In

The house I live in
a plot of earth, a street
. . .the people that I meet.
Frank Sinatra

Out for a drive one day we noticed that a wooded area had been cleared a few miles away from our house. We drove past it often after that and each time our curiosity grew. Heavy equipment moved in to contour the land, dig trenches for sewers and gas lines, lay road beds, all the infrastructure for a new community.

As soon as the roads were drivable, we went in and discovered interesting curves and courts instead of the usual grid in new developments. They stretched around the only building left standing when they cleared the area. That was Henry Ford's stable and it would become the community house. It stood in the middle of what was left of an apple orchard, next to a pond. A swimming pool went in on the other side of it. Foundations for five homes backed up to that compound. The circular road that surrounded the area had been Henry's horse track.

We discovered that the architect who designed the

15

community was the father of a little girl I baby sat many years earlier. He had helped me with algebra when I was in high school. Some say small world. I say it was a sign that we were in the right place. I felt like he had designed it just for me.

My husband and I were among the crowd that attended the grand opening to visit the models. All the projected two hundred homes were sold that week or very soon thereafter. We chose the middle house, middle in size and price. It had three bedrooms, one-and-a-half baths, and a large family kitchen. We chose a large lot so we could someday attach a garage and a family room. We scraped together the deposit and went about getting the down payment and the mortgage. We had months to do this as our house was being built.

We moved in on the fourth of July, a month before our third child was born. We had found the perfect place to raise our family. There was the pool to swim in with a lifeguard who welcomed kids alone as soon as they could swim across the pool–we had some very young swimmers. There was a pond to fish in where the kids brought home what they caught in buckets, then went back to throw them in again. I think the fish thought that was part of their dinner. There were woods and the Rouge river where the kids had adventures out of the view of parents. We heard about some of these exploits after they grew up and were glad we didn't know about them at the time. The clubhouse was the site of dance lessons, boy scout meetings, and social gatherings. The elementary school was adjacent to the community and so the school yard was available for ball games and other outdoor activities.

Best of all it was the village that it takes to raise a family. We all watched out for all the kids. On the Fourth of July, there was a kid's bike parade: an abundance of red, white and blue crepe paper adorning a variety of conveyances led by the middle school band playing Sousa marches. It was followed by hot dogs and ice cream and the dads' ball game at the schoolyard, then a pot luck dinner on the street in front of the community house that evening. We had Halloween parties before trick or treating, New Year's Eve dinner parties for the parents, and celebrations of all sorts. There were pool parties in the summer with contests for the kids and for the adults a luau with food and drink. Lifetime friendships were formed in that community and the grown-up kids still reminisce about good times in River Oaks.

Many years later my second husband and I–empty nesters–followed nearly the same pattern choosing our condo in downtown Dearborn. It was time to leave the River Oaks house, time to downsize. We had toured stacked condos in Royal Oak. They were row houses, three stories high, a large two-floor apartment built over a small one-floor and the garages. I loved them but Royal Oak was geographically unacceptable. They were too far from the office and the schools where I taught. I wished we had them in Dearborn.

Then one day a sign went up in downtown Dearborn with a picture of a very similar row of houses. Soon a trailer moved in to serve as the office and showroom. We went in to see the plans and the layout of the buildings, put our name on the list of prospective buyers, then watched as the ground was prepared, foundations went in, and buildings took shape.

When they called us, we went in to select our unit. There were six buildings surrounding a courtyard. We were the first residents to move in to the end unit of the first one finished. Some local dignitaries came to our door for a photo op with a welcome basket chock full of goodies from local businesses. The picture appeared in the local paper that week.

That same year we bought our house in Tucson in preparation for retirement. This time we did not have the privilege of watching it being built. At the time we were not even looking for a house. We were renting an apartment on the east side. Then one day we dropped off some out-of-town friends at their hotel on the west side and saw a sign for a new subdivision.

"Let's go look," I said.

It was another neighborhood laid out in curves and courts built in the foothills at the edge of the Catalinas.

"Let's look at the models,"

They were beautifully furnished but a bit larger than what we had in mind.

"I have a smaller model but its not finished yet," said the saleswoman. "Would you like to see it?"

Of course we would. I looked out at the mountains from the angled kitchen window of the roughed-in house. "We'll take it."

"We'll think about it," my husband said.

"No. We'll buy it." And we did. The next day.

The day after that we flew home to Michigan and did not see the house again for almost three months. We faxed diagrams of details for the kitchen back and forth with the interior designer who oversaw changes we asked for.

When we returned to close on the house, it was perfect. We moved in but we had to return to work a few days later and did not actually live in it until January..

On the first morning in our new house we woke up to the most gorgeous sunrise I have ever seen. The sky and the Catalinas turned fiery red.

What a welcome!

Warnings

The worst moments in life are heralded
by small observations.
Andy Weir, *The Martian*

Red lights, road signs, sirens. Those are the easy signs of danger. The harder ones are the premonitions we have of difficulties ahead. I often recognize those signs in hindsight and wish I had paid more attention to my body. Like the hackles on a dog's back when he senses threats, we have forebodings or hunches we often don't recognize until it's too late.

When I noticed that Jerry was sleeping more than usual, I paid little attention until he markedly lost vitality, the only symptom of what would follow. I had heard of valley fever and for some reason I googled it. One of the symptoms noted was a rash on the legs. I rushed out to the living room.

"Take down your pants," I said.. No rash, not valley fever. Actually the rash comes later.

When the exhaustion continued and he was noticeably weaker, we headed to urgent care. X-rays indicated pneumonia, so they sent him home with antibiotics. After a week he was no better. In fact he was hardly able to get out of bed. This time we went to the emergency room, where tests indicated failing heart, kidneys and liver. He was admitted that night. Two days later when we thought he was dying, the pulmonologist diagnosed valley fever and began treating him with anti-fungals. He began to feel better by the next morning. Two days later he was well enough to return home. Recovery was slow, but a couple of months later, he was nearly back to normal, swimming again and working on his stamina.

This had all happened in Arizona. Valley fever is a desert disease caused by breathing in spores of a fungus rising from disturbed soil. Most cases are mild, simple flu-like symptoms. But about two per cent are severe enough for hospitalization.

Back in Michigan, where valley fever is unknown, Jerry began to have drenching night sweats. The doctor seemed unconcerned and brushed off my suggestion of valley fever. She sent him to the lab for more tests. Then he had repeated bouts of gout, which they treated with prednisone, a drug that compromises the immune system.

After a couple of months, this all culminated in one of the worst possible effects of the fungus: coccimeningitis. The fungus gets into the spinal cord. It affects only one per cent of valley fever patients and kills thirty five per cent of them. Thankfully not him, but he spent seventeen days in the hospital, another six weeks in home care, and several months before he was back to normal. He will take anti-fungals for the rest of his life with frequent blood draws to check his tolerance for the drug. For about a year he was susceptible to every illness that came around.

I look back and wonder what inkling caused me to google valley fever before any of this happened. If I had asked the urgent care doctor about it, would they have treated him early enough to prevent such drastic results? The antibiotics he prescribed exacerbated the condition by introducing more fungus into his system. So did all the prednisone.

Hindsight.

What's In a Name?

Of course, a sign doesn't mean anything unless
you know how to interpret it.
Arthur Golden
Memoirs of a Geisha

Every five years Jerry and I review our will and our trust in light of any changes in the law and our own circumstances, we talk to the kids about our wishes for our final days, and we check out future housing. Our plan was to move into a senior residence at age 85. That plan changed when the valley fever struck.

It was time to think seriously about advancing our plans for senior living by a few years and we began our search in earnest.

We toured several facilities both in Michigan and in Arizona.. They ranged from dreary places where residents were waiting to die–God's waiting room according to one resident–to resort-style places, more like hotels than homes.

We were already familiar with The Fountains in Tucson and liked the atmosphere. There was a buzz of activity in the air. We met Jerry's cousin's nephew who was the manager at that time. We had lunch there. The food was delicious. A few years after that initial visit, we began to attend Elder Circles there and met some of the residents. It felt like the place for us, so we made an appointment for a tour.

We had a cordial visit with Gloria, a young enthusiastic sales rep who had worked at two other senior communities in the course of her career. We compared our opinions of these places and agreed that the best choice for us was The Fountains. We put our names on the waiting list for a two bedroom apartment, on the third floor, facing east, with a view of the Catalinas, specifically one of four apartments. Our target date was to move in in two years.

A week or so later we had our annual visit with our financial advisor at Fidelity. Jason told us about a new type of annuity that they offered. We could convert our IRA's to this fund, which would provide a monthly income that coincidentally would be just the amount of our monthly fees at The Fountains. A good sign. Everything was falling into place.

It reminded me of Elaine's experience. Elaine was my daughter-in-law's mom, and our family had more or less adopted her when my son Joe and Julie moved to California. She had Parkinson's disease and needed to be in a setting with more support available. But she was resisting. She wanted to be near her daughter even though she did not like California, and she was physically unable to manage the complications of the move–or even the flight from Michigan–by herself. Besides that, Joe and Julie's living situation was tenuous. They didn't know where they would be in another few months. And Elaine did not want to sell her condo, which was not worth what she'd paid for it because of the recession. She needed a push, which the family provided to help her make her decision. Then circumstances–the universe?– intervened.

Julie was in town for a few days so she helped her mom search for a place and make arrangements for the sale of her condo. They found a lovely apartment at Walton Woods which would be available at the end of the month, no waiting list. Her condo sold in three days for $5,000.00 more than the asking price. Julie would be free to return the next month to help her mother with all the details of the move. I saw all this as a sign that she was on the right path.

As for us, after our visit with Gloria, she gave us her card. Her last name was Livingood. We knew we were in the right place.

Wishes, Desires and Prayers

===

Once you make a decision, the universe
conspires to make it happen.
Ralph Waldo Emerson

Be Careful What You Ask For

Ask and it shall be given unto you.
Jesus

As I gazed out the bedroom window of our new apartment at The Fountains, my view of the Catalinas was partially blocked by a branch of a palo verde. It was an awkward thing sticking out the side of the tree. *I wish they would cut that off,* I mused. A few days later I looked out the same window and the branch was gone. I didn't know my wishes were that powerful.

Then one Sunday for dinner we had falling-off-the-bone-tender braised lamb shanks. A week or so earlier I had seen a box of frozen prepared lamb shanks at Costco and thought of one of my favorite meals that I cooked when I could occasionally find them at Safeway. *We'll never have those at The Fountains,* I thought. I was wrong. I hadn't even wished for them, just remembered how I liked them, and there they were on our Sunday menu complete with mint jelly.

The most life changing answer to a prayer happened many years ago. Soon after Jerry and I were married–the second time for both of us–with nine kids to support and very little money, I sat down to write our monthly checks. It was a sunny spring morning, the air fresh, the garden beginning to flower, but I was literally spent. The balance in the checkbook was pitifully low.

"God, I'm tired of being poor. I want to be rich." I said it out loud, not really a prayer, a cry of desperation. That out of my system, I went on with my day until Jerry came home a few hours later.

"I got fired," he announced. *That was not exactly what I had in mind, God*, I thought.

Several years later I looked back and saw that that was the first step in a journey leading to my prayer's answer. We spent six months eking out our living with whatever money we could lay our hands on from my part time teaching and a few commissions from Jerry's sales as well as unemployment compensation.

Again on a sunny day in the very same room, with the same desperation I wailed, "We have enough food for a week, then I don't know what we'll do. You have to find a job."

I opened the newspaper to the want ads and there was an ad for an industrial battery salesman for Exide Corporation. We had to have that job. We figured out to the penny what we needed to live on. That was the salary Jerry asked for. He had already lost a similar opportunity to another salesman by asking for too much money. This time he got the job.

"I should have asked for more," he grumbled. I was just happy to know we would have a pay check even though we wouldn't get rich on that amount.

The next step on the journey came on a snowy day in winter. His associate who was to attend a meeting in Hilton Head took sick. Jerry went in his place. A new product was introduced there that would be our key to the riches I had asked for. Jerry saw the future of Uninterruptible Power Supplies, backup power for the room-sized computers in operation at that time. He came back fired up to sell them and was immediately successful, increasing his commissions.

When Exide Electronics split off from the battery division and decided to sell through reps rather than company salesmen, Jerry and I started our own manufacturer's rep business. It was seven years after that prayer before we had enough money to call ourselves well off.

But there was a price to pay. I had been teaching part time at two local colleges. When a full time position opened in one of them, we thought it was the answer to our prayers. A full time salary with benefits would help while our fledgling business grew profitable. I didn't get the position. That resulted in a discrimination suit–more about that later. I was needed at the office, so I had to give up teaching, a job I loved. I did win the suit and four years later received what I would have earned until retirement had I continued to teach.

The next step was the realization of one of Jerry's dreams. Detroit Edison was spinning off Powerscan, its battery repair group, and he wanted to own part of it. One of our salespeople mentioned the name of the man who would probably win out over other competitors for the purchase of the company. He needed help to make the down payment. Jerry called him and set up a meeting. The settlement money from my lawsuit came just in time to purchase a major share of the stock. That turned out to be the investment that guaranteed our retirement.

We had always been rich in other things, family, friends, and the essentials of life. Now we had money to spend on extras and travel. I call that rich.

Trial

God works in mysterious ways.
Common Saying

The first time I saw Debby I had no idea what an important part she would play in my life. Jerry and I were sitting in the waiting room of a lawyer we were about to consult about a potential law suit. She came out of her office to greet a client, and I was impressed by her greeting, her smile, her firm handshake, her air of self-confidence.

But let's go back to what brought us there. In August of 1982, I was turned down for a full-time teaching position at Henry Ford Community College. The position was a perfect fit for my credentials in communication. The announcement had been written by my retiring mentor, probably with me in mind. I had been teaching there part-time for eight years, but they chose a man who was clearly less qualified. I had a PhD. He had an MA and ABD (all but dissertation). His teaching experience had been high school math and science in a rural setting. His only qualification for teaching speech communication was coaching debate, an activity not included in the job description. I suspected gender discrimination and set out to prove it. I went to the

Equal Employment Opportunity Commission to file a complaint and begin the process.

My intake officer at the EEOC welcomed me warmly and I knew she and I were compatible when I noticed the unicorns decorating her office. I like unicorns. She suggested that I do some research and return the next day, early, so that I could meet with her and not with whoever was on rotation that day. She was very interested in my case.

I talked to my mentor and my former advisor at Wayne State where the man who got the position was doing his doctoral work and coaching debate. Jim told me about him and even provided me with the man's personnel file. He also told me that the man had not originally applied for the position but was brought in by a member of the search committee. That was suspicious to say the least.

Later one evening before a class I was teaching, I was talking casually to a colleague, a member of the committee that made the hiring decision. As we talked he said that I had not been his first choice for the position because he preferred a younger man! Big mistake on his part.

At the EEOC everything proceeded smoothly. The staff who questioned both the college lawyers and me at a hearing was thorough and even-handed. They would determine if and how to proceed. A month later I was still awaiting their judgment. I became impatient so I called and was told that I should hear soon. A month later I called again and was told that I had been given a new case officer and he would call sooon.. Another month went by and I didn't hear from him. It seemed that the whole process had come to an end. That was the year that Clarence Thomas was appointed to take over the EEOC and everything stopped. Two more months and I decided to pursue the matter on my own.

I made an appointment with a discrimination lawyer recommended by my former advisor. That brought us to the waiting room where I first saw Debby. I could see the lawyer we would be talking to through the open door of his office. He was smoking a cigar. He put it out when we came in but his office reeked of cigar smoke. I explained why we were there.

He leaned back in his chair and said to my husband, "We don't want this case to go to court. We'll work for a settlement."

That's what you think, I thought, *I want these people to answer for what they did.* He continued to address my husband and paid very little attention to me. Big mistake. I was the complainant..

When we got in the car, I asked Jerry what he thought. With a twinkle in his eye and his silly smirk, he said, "I think he's not for us." He knew very well what I thought. He is a salesman, good at reading people, especially my feminist attitudes.

At home I called another lawyer known for discrimination work. He was not available but one of his associates talked to me at some length, and we made an appointment for our first conference. She turned out to be Debby, the lawyer we had seen in the waiting room of the other lawyer. She was now in a different office with a different firm.

I told her I had gone to the EEOC because I thought that Henry Ford might reconsider and offer me a job. Two-thirds of their teaching staff was part-time. They certainly could have hired me if they chose to, or so I thought. Clearly that was not going to happen. In that case I wanted to face them in front of a judge and jury.

"We will go to court," she said after hearing my story. That's what I wanted to hear.

Debby and I worked together putting all the information in order and we filed suit in April. Depositions were taken and various hearings were held over the next few months. And once more I discovered how the universe conspires to give me what I want.

The Circuit Court, where they handle civil cases in Michigan, was in overflow at the time. Work had been farmed out to other courts and so our mediation hearing was held in a local district court. There the judge looked at the discrepancy between the college's offer and our demand, and passed it back to Circuit Court without even trying to work it out. The whole suit might have been stopped there if they had made an offer worth considering. Or at any time if they simply said they didn't like me. There is no law against that.

The case went from there to Recorder's Court–where criminal cases are heard–for jury selection. Our judge was one of the most conservative judges on the bench. Sitting in the courtroom I heard him yell in chambers, "Not in my court you won't!" The defense had planned to ask for astrological signs of potential jurors. He oversaw the selection of six jurors, no alternates, and sent us on to the chief judge of Recorders Court where the trial was eventually held.

Ordinarily all of this would have been under the purview of one judge and that judge would have pushed for settlement. Instead, because each judge had passed it on to the next judge in a different court, we went to trial.

On the scheduled day, when everyone concerned was gathered in the hallway outside the courtroom, the judge came out to tell us he could not begin our trial that day because he had not completed his current case as was expected. He

33

apologized for the inconvenience. I was impressed with his concern for the jurors. He could have sent a deputy to give us the message.

When we appeared in court the next week, there were only five jurors. One had been excused to care for a dying relative. Fine with me. I had reservations about the woman excused. She held an authority position in a youth organization and I thought she might see me as a trouble-making employee rather than a wronged professional. Was this a god shot? Another one of God's mysterious ways?

The trial took two weeks and I got my wish to face the responsible faculty members. A couple of them visibly squirmed on the stand. They had apparently falsified at least one record. They did their best to discredit me, but the jury believed me, thanks to the skillful questioning of Debby. They awarded me what I would have earned teaching until retirement.

The court situation was not the only factor in giving me what I wanted. The college itself contributed. They had not consulted their insurance company when the suit was filed. That would surely have resulted in a settlement. (Insurance companies know better than to leave their fate in the hands of unpredictable jurors.) Instead they turned to a law firm that convinced them they could not lose, and they chose to defend their decision. When they lost of course, the insurance company declined to pay the judgment.

It took two more years and an appeal–six years since it all started--before we received the money. Money was not my objective but that is the language of the law. That gave us what we needed to realize my husband's dream of owning Powerscan. We became major stockholders in the company and that paid for our very comfortable retirement.

Who Knows Best?

You can't always get what you want
But if you try sometime you find
You get what you need.
The Rolling Stones

I don't always get what I want but I do always get what I need. That's my version of the song. For me trying just gets in the way. It's better to welcome whatever I find with the joy of discovery.

When the time came for moving to a senior retirement community, or as my husband calls it, "the home," we had been searching for the right place for twenty years. We had visited friends in some of them, taken tours, gone to open houses, lectures, and various events usually involving lunch or refreshments of some kind. We had looked in Michigan. We had looked in Arizona where we were snowbirds for years. Our family was in Michigan. Our hearts were in Arizona. We followed our hearts.

We wanted to be in a place with lots of activity, good food, and interesting people. We wanted staff who did not patronize their residents, calling them sweetie or protecting them by not providing stoves in their kitchens for fear of fire. We did not want to be assigned tables and times in the dining room. One place we visited was proud that meals were served at 8:00, 12:00, and 5:00 and everyone ate at the same time, at the same tables. It seemed to us that most of our time there would be spent getting ready for another meal. We wanted flexibility and our choice of dinner partners. We wanted a kitchen where we could actually cook if we so chose, not just a microwave and a mini refrigerator. We wanted an attractive apartment with unobtrusive safety measures. We wanted a good library with residents actually using it. Not a place where people were waiting to die. We wanted The Fountains.

In the fall of 2012 we put our names on the waiting list for an apartment with a target date of moving in in October, 2014. We chose the apartment we wanted, two bedrooms, two baths. Specifically we hoped for the end unit on the third floor of the building facing east with a view of the Catalinas and even a partial view of the city lights at night if we ever stayed up that late.

In the spring of 2014, Gloria told us that the apartment we wanted would probably be available soon. The problem was that two other residents also wanted it and they had preference over us newcomers.

"I do have another one I'd like you to see," she said. "You probably won't like it but come look anyway."

Why not? She took us to the northern end of the building on the first floor. Seriously? The location was the exact opposite of what we had chosen. We followed her down the hall and into an apartment with a view of the Catalinas. It was newly remodeled with wood floors, new stainless and black appliances, attractive cupboards and counters, and contemporary brushed nickel light fixtures. And then the clincher: the door wall opened to a patio opposite the area where our car would be parked. We would be able to come and go without the elevators and long halls we had in our Michigan high rise.

We are fringers, that is we tend to stay on the edges of groups. We sit in the last row at movies, the side tables at dinner functions, the front row at lectures. Our condo had been an end unit next to the railroad tracks in Dearborn. It was considered less desirable than those on the courtyard but I saw the proximity of parking for guests and a clear view of both the sunrise and the sunset. The trains were of no consequence. We didn't even hear them after a while.

This apartment was perfect for us. Furthermore they could hold it for ninety days and even reduce the rent until we returned from our summer in Michigan.

We looked at each other. "We'll take it," we said.

"What about the wood floors?" Gloria asked. "You wanted carpet."

I had already picked colors for walls and carpet in case an apartment came up while we were in Michigan.

" I can live with them," I said. I had hardly noticed the floors in light of the other advantages.

"You should probably think about it. Call me tomorrow."

When one of our Arizona friends heard our plans, she was aghast. "You're moving in in August? Do you know what Tucson is like in August? No one moves in August."

I had an idea of what it's like. I knew temperatures would be in the hundreds, but it's dry heat. That means it's like an oven, not a steam bath. I looked forward to the monsoon, which is what they call the summer rains. The electrical storms over the mountains are spectacular.

The Golden Rule

*Do not do to others what angers you if done
to you by others.*
Socrates

Protocol. I did not want to write up a request. I did
not want to seek out Nicole in the office so that she could take
it to the Board. I did not want to wait for their decision, then
wait even longer for Nicole to call and report their approval
back to me. I knew they would approve it.

All I wanted was to use the chapel in our apartment
building for the next meeting of our Elder Circle. It would be
much easier just to gather there without official approval. It's
always open for the use of residents. In the unlikely case that
someone else would be using it on the day I wanted it, we
could simply return to our own place in the board room.

I was still dithering about what to do when I opened
our apartment door and a flier fell to the floor. It was an
announcement for the newly redecorated chapel and its use:
the regular rosaries and Bible studies, memorials, and even a
few concerts as well as personal meditations. The notice was
from the chapel committee which is now in charge of
scheduling. Turns out a member of the committee is also a

member of our Elder Circle. Problem solved. Betty would take care of it and she did.

I wanted to use the chapel because we would be talking about the Golden Rule. There are six quilted panels on the walls, trees in restful greens. One is embroidered with a welcome. On each of the others is the Golden Rule as stated in the five major religions: Christian, Jewish, Muslim, Hindu, and Buddhist. There has been some discontent that there is no crucifix. Formerly the decor had been very Catholic. Now it is non-sectarian.

Karen Armstrong, the brilliant scholar and former nun, tells us that all religions are based on the Golden Rule. Five hundred years before Jesus, Confucius taught his followers this guiding principle: "Do not impose on others what you do not wish for yourself."

Karen gave her version in her TED talk: "Look into your own heart, discover what it is that gives you pain and then refuse, under any circumstance whatsoever, to inflict that pain on anybody else."

The Jewish Virtual Library quotes this story from the Babylonian Talmud:

> "Once there was a gentile who came before Shammai, and said to him: "Convert me on the condition that you teach me the whole Torah while I stand on one foot. Shammai pushed him aside with the measuring stick he was holding. The same fellow came before Hillel, and Hillel converted him, saying: That which is despicable to you, do not do to your fellow, this is the whole Torah, and the rest is commentary, go and learn it."

We held our circle in the chapel that day thanks to Betty and her committee. We had those beautiful panels to illuminate our discussion. And the members liked it so much that the chapel is now their regular meeting place.

Tuning In

*The greatest tragedy of human experience
is not to live in time, in both senses of that phrase.*
Christian Wiman

Shopping

Instructions for living a life.
Pay attention.
Be astonished.
Tell about it.
Mary Oliver

What drew me to Michael's that day? I had been restless and needed something to do besides read and watch TV during my free hours. I needed a project. My arthritic fingers could no longer manage a fine needle for embroidery, but unlike Grandma Moses who turned to a paint brush, I turned to knitting. I could hold large sized knitting needles.

We would need an afghan for our new apartment so I planned to go to our local knit shop for inspiration. Then in the course of our travels, I happened into Michael's. I didn't know it was the last day of their yarn event, but there was the yarn I had visualized, shades of blue and green to blend with our planned color scheme. $1.99 per skein instead of the usual $3.49. I had my project.

Michael's was not one of my usual haunts. I would go there only when I needed something specific. That day it was a vague notion some would call intuition. I call it being in

43

tune with the universe. When I pay attention to the ordinary, everyday necessities of living, I find the world full of wonder, and in the case of shopping, just what I need whether I know it or not.

I am not a shop-til-you-drop kind of shopper but I am an inveterate bargain hunter. Only occasionally impulsive, I usually think twice before buying, especially anything major. Unless it's a bargain too good to resist. My mother always said I could smell a bargain. I am just glad I can recognize one when I see it.

When I needed new bedding to replace our worn sheets, I went to Meiers, a Target-type store in Michigan, and headed for the linen department. I walked past several shelves of various bed sets, mostly queens and kings. I needed a full. Of course color was important to go with the duvet and shams we already had. Then on a nearly empty clearance shelf, I found exactly what I needed, a sage green high quality sheet set. It seemed to be sitting alone on the shelf almost as if a spotlight shone on it. With that good luck I went on to look for a new bed skirt and found the only dark blue, full-bed size skirt in the store, on sale of course. Wow.

Many of my purchases are serendipitous but some are planned, like the leather recliners that we wanted for our apartment. Their price was outrageous but they were so-o-o comfortable. We resisted the extravagance.

A few months later we decided to heck with it; they would be our Christmas presents to ourselves. We went in to Copenhagen to order the chairs we wanted, only to find them on clearance. We saved $300.00 per chair, then to top it off we were eligible for the bonus they offered–for a limited time only–with the purchase of two chairs. We could choose $750.00 worth of Stressless accessories to go with the chairs.

We chose a side table and a small attached tray for Jer's chair, things we would never have bought at their regular price.

One day when we were driving by the Sam Levitz furniture store, I suggested we drop in and see what they had on sale. They always have a sale going on for one reason or another. We checked out the clearance area first and found a table and four chairs at an irresistible price. As the salesman filled out the paperwork, I wandered through the store looking at other stuff. All the couches were too big and bulky for our room. And the seats were too wide for me to sit on comfortably without a pillow. Then in the middle of a crowded grouping, a blue couch beckoned. I sat down and was embraced by a comfy cushioned seat, just the right size and color. It turned out to be one of Levitz's Doorbusters which meant a rock bottom price.

We still needed a coffee table and end tables, but we were in no hurry. We had the essentials. Then, the day before the movers came, we discovered Home Styles Gallery, a consignment shop not far from the apartment. We toured the whole store and when we had almost given up hope, there they were crowded into a group of living room pieces. The perfect tables. Contemporary. Solid wood with glass tops over shelves that would hold a load of books and magazines and anything else we wanted to keep in reach..

The sales woman stood by watching us and commented, "They're Copenhagen you know."

I could tell. They would go perfectly with our chairs and couch. And the price was unbelievably low, not even a quarter of what they would have cost new. The next day the movers picked them up at the store to add to the rest of our furniture saving us the delivery charge. Our living room was complete except for one little thing.

The next week we were on our way to the Fidelity office when we passed another shop. It was run by The Girls, a group of women who manage estate sales, then take any unsold items to sell in their shop.

"Let's go in," I said, and we did.

There in the back, under a pile of stuff, Jer spied the perfect entry table for our Hopi Kachinas and our Navajo and Mata Ortiz pottery. It was just the right size, smaller than most, rustic pine with small bright-colored tiles around the edge. When we went to pay for it, they took twenty five per cent off the already low price. It was a sale day.

Timing is everything.

Daffodils

The litter of breakfast remains,
milk bottomed bowls
peanut butter smears
stray cereal flakes
toast crusts
sticky jam
knives spoons
jars here and there
echoes of squabbling
children, and
in the center
a bowl of daffodils.

If she could focus on the flowers
ignore the chaos in her head
perhaps . . . .just perhaps
she could escape sliding
into the abyss
that paralyzing darkness.

Unfortunately she could not. That evening she signed in to a mental hospital. But that's the end of this story. It began with a phone call.

"Gerry, we're going to have to postpone lunch. I'm not going in to the office today."

Susan and I had planned on lunch in downtown Detroit where she worked as a copy writer for the *Free Press* and wrote book reviews. She had recently written a full-page feature article on her experience with mental illness. She was bi-polar.

"Why don't I come over and we can eat someplace near you?" I suggested.

She gave me directions to her house. It would be a forty-five-minute drive. "I'm going to shower and wash my hair. I should be there in about an hour and a half."

Susan and I knew each other from meetings of Detroit Women Writers. During manic phases of her disease she wrote powerful, imaginative poetry. We planned on reading our poetry to each other after lunch.

As we ate, the subject of Jer's sister came up. She was in a mental institution, heavily drugged after a major schizophrenic episode. She had made several half-hearted attempts at suicide.

"One morning the paper boy discovered her lying in the snow in her nightgown," I told Susan. "Another time she tried to hang herself on a tree in the back yard on a branch too flimsy to bear her weight."

"One of the problems with mental illness is the inability to plan and execute an effective action," Susan said "We just don't think through the consequences of our actions."

She paused for a moment, then added. "And I'm not always fully aware of my surroundings." I remembered once when we were heading to our cars after a meeting, I grabbed her arm to stop her from walking out into traffic.

After lunch, we went back to her house to read our poetry. We discussed our work, comfortably offering suggestions where they were called for. It was a normal, productive workshop for two.

At about three o'clock her pastor dropped in. I left for home, glad to be on the road before rush hour. It had been a pleasant afternoon. Later I learned that she was admitted to the mental ward that evening.

A month or so after that we saw each other at another meeting. Susan thanked me for my visit.

"When I talked to you on the phone," she said, "you said you were going to shower. I told myself I could do that too and I did. You helped me to get through the day. I don't know what I would have done if you had not been with me."

I was clearly tuned in that day. Ordinarily I would have suggested rescheduling our lunch. I certainly would not have driven to the other end of town for lunch with a friend I was not particularly close to. I was needed and I went.

Connections

===============

*No man is an island entire of itself; every man
is a piece of the continent, a part of the main . . .*
John Donne

Free Lunch

Rule #39: There is no such thing as coincidence.
Leroy Jethro Gibbs, NCIS

If you hang out with AA members or even go to a meeting–there are open meetings for non-members–you will hear them talk about god shots. Other people call them coincidences and do or do not believe in them. People who reject the idea of divine intervention prefer the term "synchronicity." The parallel universe? Whatever you call them, they happen to all of us.

A major one in my life happened in my eightieth year. It was time for our annual financial checkup. In Michigan we had attended an unimpressive presentation by a financial advisor at Andiamo's, a fine Italian restaurant close to our apartment in Dearborn. We wasted two hours at the follow-up appointment where we learned more than we wanted to know about the presenter but nothing about how he would increase our return and lower our fees. His recommendations would cost $200.00 and probably waste another two hours of our time. We ignored his phone calls after that.

We returned to Tucson and made an appointment with Jason, our Fidelity advisor. He introduced us to a new annuity product that impressed us. It differed from other annuities which take all of your money in exchange for an income guaranteed for life. The insurance company reaps the reward of any increase in the value of the principal. In the Fidelity plan our money remains ours and *we* receive any increase in value and the consequent increase in future income. The income is guaranteed whatever the market conditions. It can only go up. We signed the papers to convert our retirement accounts to the new plan two days before the stock market crashed. Lucky us. We had thirty days to make changes if necessary.

Then our friends the Siegels invited us to another financial presentation. This one at Fleming's. How could we resist? After a fabulous melt-in-your-mouth steak dinner and an impressive presentation by Stuart, a charismatic young man, we made an appointment for a review of our finances. Unlike our hapless Michigan advisor, Stuart gathered all our information and made an appointment to report back to us the next week. Free. We would have something to compare to the Fidelity plan.

I thought all was in order financially when it all exploded. Stuart came with his critique of the annuity we had just bought and presented us an alternative. We still had two weeks to back out of the Fidelity plan. What he told us was convincing.

"The VIP investment group will control 60% of your funds and it is a 'turrible' fund," he said. "There's little chance of increasing your value using just Fidelity funds. And," he added, "the costs are actually higher than they say."

He pulled out impressive charts showing that his plan would increase our income by about $9,000.00 per year. We were hooked. We signed the papers to put the plan into motion. Of course the next day we had second thoughts and decided to look into the matter before proceeding. When will we ever remember to sleep on whatever we want to buy?

We sat down at the computer with our good friend Google. We found a barrage of insurance agents and companies selling annuities as well as alerts to prospective buyers. Clearly there is a lot of money to be made in the annuity business. We gave our email address and phone number to two agencies for information and comparison of rates and had immediate responses. What we did not find was any mention of the "venerable old" company Stuart was selling. I looked that up and found that in April the company had been bought by the Harbinger Group which is run by a billionaire hedge fund owner.

"They need cash," said my business savvy husband. So that was the reason for the incentive that would increase our income so much.

Jer went on to check on the performance of the Fidelity VIP fund that Stuart claimed was "turrible" and found it was not at all terrible. Besides that, it was only a temporary fund for the first sixty days that the plan was in effect, then the annuity group would take over and make the investments. They performed superbly. My head was spinning with information.

Now for the god shot. We had talked to Stuart on Thursday. On Friday–the day we hit the internet–he called to say he needed the policies to return to Fidelity to include with the letters of instruction and the forms we had signed to return the money to our account. He would send a FedEx envelope in which to return them. He had neglected to take the policies with him on Friday. That mistake saved us from a financial disaster. A god shot.

We returned to Fidelity the next week to talk to their insurance expert. We spent an hour with him comparing Stuart's policy to theirs. He pointed out the differences and the misinformation that Stuart had given us. We had made the right choice in the first place.

As we were walking out the door of his office he casually asked, "Do you know what his commission would be?"

We turned back.

With a Cheshire smile he said, "$68,000.00."

How It Works

*Doing the will of God leaves me no time
for disputing about His plans.*
George MacDonald

Why does "God's plan" make me uncomfortable? Not the plan, the words. I have to translate "God" to "universe" and then I'm okay. When I hear "God's plan," it suggests to me that God is responsible for anything that happens. We humans are off the hook. That's not how I see the world. I see us living in a web of people helping each other through life. We find God in each other and in ourselves. We do God's work.

I first noticed this web when my father died. When he was gone my world fell apart. My mother was unable to cope and could not go back to their home without the company of friends. She bounced around from place to place for almost two years, finally moving to Florida to be close to her brother and sister. Good friends of ours divorced after close to fifty years of marriage. My husband and I were separated within the year and eventually divorced. It was as though my father held us all together like a rubber band and when it snapped, we went off in all directions.

When my son Steve had an accident, the connections were even more startling. We were winding up a day at the lake with Jerry's family. The boat and dock were buttoned up; the laundry gathered; the car packed. It was only four-thirty but we were due in Lansing for a gathering at my brother's house at six   I was putting away the last of the dishes downstairs in the kitchen when I heard a commotion upstairs and Steve's buddy Dave yelling.

The only word I heard was "accident." I dashed up the stairs in time to see the bathroom door slam behind Dave's back. I stood outside the door, dish towel in hand, and waited anxiously to hear what had happened. Dave came out of the bathroom looking confused. He was in a state of shock. His glasses were broken so he could not see clearly. The back seam of his pants was split from top to bottom. His story came out in gasps as Jerry grabbed keys and wallet and we ran for the car.

"Mark's car hit a tree . . . Steve was driving . . . two women . . . drove me . . . back here."

Dave didn't know exactly where the accident had happened and he couldn't see well enough to recognize the roads. They all looked alike as country roads do. We guessed where it might have happened and drove frantically down various roads around the cottage. It had to be Hankerd. We arrived at the accident scene where the county sheriff's crew was cleaning up the area. They directed us to follow after the ambulance already on its way to Ann Arbor .

"The kids are OK," called one of the men. If I had seen the car, I would not have believed him. My protective blindness kicked in. I did not see it. My only thought was the kids. I clung to the sheriff's words as we raced to the hospital.

We found Steve moaning on a gurney in an emergency room cubicle. "Why me?" he mumbled. "Why me?" Then he closed his eyes and stopped breathing. I panicked and called for a nurse. By the time she arrived he had shuddered and begun his labored breathing again.

"He has a broken rib," she said.. " It makes breathing painful but he's in no danger. The plastic surgeon is on his way."

Steve's injuries were mostly facial, a long jagged cut between his lower lip and his chin where his teeth had penetrated and broken off on the steering wheel. It took the doctor a couple of hours to stitch his chin.

While he was in surgery we checked on the other kids and talked to the parents who had arrived by then. Three of the kids were shaken up and bruised but otherwise all right. Andrea, in the passenger seat, was the most seriously injured. She suffered a trauma to her back that kept her hospitalized for several days and in a brace for several months.

After surgery the doctor came in and said they were keeping Steve overnight because of concerns that his lung had been punctured by the broken rib. They released him the next day when it was determined that the puncture was a quick in and out that left no damage.

Steve told us the story of the accident as we drove home. "I was driving. Mark didn't know the roads. You know that curve on Hankerd?"

"Yes."

"I said, 'Watch out. Around this bend a tree jumps out in front of us.'"

Andrea thought he was kidding so she played along and quickly buckled her seat belt. That may have saved her life. Over the rise and around the curve, the worn tires of

Mark's old Mustang lost their grip on the drizzle-slicked road and the tree did indeed jump out in front of them. They hit it. How's that for premonition?

The following Friday we took Steve back to the hospital to have his stitches removed, then drove to the junkyard where the Mustang sat forlornly in its final resting place. I was horrified. I could not imagine how six-foot Steve had climbed through the side window, crushed to a slit between the caved-in roof and the squashed front end. His double-jointedness must have helped. We saw the two notches in the steering wheel where his front teeth had lodged–all that orthodontia gone to waste.

Later we found out that things were not as bad as they might have been and this is where connections become evident. The tree they hit was dead . It broke on impact and fell on the roof of the car. If the tree had been alive and strong, the consequences could have been far worse. That tree had died after being hit by my son Tim's father-in-law a couple of years earlier.

The people involved in the accident were connected in other ways. The girl in the back seat was the daughter of our lake neighbor who was Jerry's mom's art teacher. We had learned that in our get-acquainted meeting when they first moved in. Andrea turned out to be the step-daughter of a classmate of Jerry's, a girl he had dated in high school. We discovered that when we met at their twenty-fifth class reunion the next year.

The accident happened at the edge of the parking lot of a state park on Half Moon Lake. The first person on the scene was a life guard from the park. He helped get the kids out of the car and gave what first aid he could. When Steve moved into his new dorm at Michigan State the next month, he was greeted by the young man who had come to his rescue, his new resident advisor.

And Mark fared better than he might have. He had only basic insurance on his old car, but because Steve was driving, our more liberal collision coverage applied. Mark collected the market value of the car which was surprisingly high because the Mustang was a classic.

Once I recognized the existence of these person-to-person connections in life, I could see them everywhere, people helping one another knowingly or unknowingly. I am amazed and delighted at how widespread the networks of people can be and how far-reaching across time and space we influence each other. I can't help comparing this human phenomenon to quantum physics which has proved that when subatomic particles are split, they respond as a unit no matter how far they are from each other. One scientist has described this as a state of "quantum entanglement."

While I was writing this piece, I received an e-mail from my daughter Laura in Michigan. We had never used the term "God's plan" when we talked so when she used the term, it surprised me as did the series of events she described. She saw connections like those I was thinking about two thousand miles away in Arizona. The two of us were on the same wave length. Here is her e-mail, edited slightly:

. . . after 10 months of planning including 1 previous cancellation, this past weekend data center shut-down-&-refresh at the Ren Cen was a success.

Bud Parker gave his leftover Mercury megaphone

steel to Tim [her brother] in 1999 when he cleared out his work shop.

Tim remembered he had the steel and was home Saturday and answered his cell phone [a miracle in itself].

Tim has a machine shop and could cut and drill the steel Bud gave him in 1999 to quickly turn around 4 brackets that were missing for the project at the Ren Cen that I have been working on scheduling for 10 months.

Tim has friends at his airport with a press (for bending metal). They happened to be in their workshop at the airport.

Tim's friends readily and expertly bent the steel to complete making the brackets required to finish the project I had scheduled over the past 10 months.

God's plans fell into place including all of the previous steps starting in 1999 when Bud gave the steel to Tim that was used for brackets for my client RichWelch's power distribution to successfully complete the work over this past weekend. Did I mention Bud Parker taught Rich Welch how to race hydroplanes and was a mentor to Tim? And Rich Welch drove for Tim when together they smashed the world record for B class hydroplanes . . .

She went on to say that the whole process was accomplished in two and a half hours and the job was completed as scheduled. This complicated chain of events and her sending me the email at that moment can hardly be called coincidence in my book.

That's how it works.

People

People who need people are the luckiest people in the world.
Barbara Streisand

A myriad of amazing people have enriched my life, sometimes in brief encounters, sometimes in lasting friendships, sometimes temporarily when I needed them or they needed me.

I can't help smiling when I think of Victor Boner, the skip tracer I found through an article in the *Detroit Free Press*. He claimed he could find anyone anywhere for only $50.00. A detective would cost far more. I drove out to his office to see him about my errant ex-husband, who had left the country. He told me that a few phone calls and some flowers for secretaries accounted for his success. When I got back to my office about forty-five minutes later, there was a message to call him. He had the information. A follow up article a month or so later reported that Mr. Boner had disappeared, ducking a huge telephone bill.

One day Jerry and I shared a table at Costco eating hot dogs with the former president of the Frank Lloyd Wright School of Architecture at Taliesin West. He lived in Scottsdale, which he called Snotsdale, and bemoaned the

64

crumbling of this unique school as the new board sought accreditation.

We met another Lloyd in an Ames, Iowa, coffee shop where we ate delicious black bean burgers and shared a fruit smoothie. He told us about the international Nevil Shute Society which he had discovered in Australia when he was there for a wedding. Of course we talked about one of Jer's favorite books: *Trustee From a Tool Room*. A pleasant pause on our drive to Arizona.

They were just two of the interesting people we have enjoyed in chance encounters. And then there was Ken. We struck up a conversation at an Arizona Theatre Company production and he became a dear friend, going so far as to pick us up at the Phoenix airport late one night when we were stranded due to the ice in Albuquerque that cancelled our Tucson flight. He was my resource person for almost anything until he died quietly one night when he sat down with his daughter to watch a Netflix movie.

I learned my life lessons from deeper relationships. Gramma taught me that I am safe in the cradle of God's love. Miss Brandt, my kindergarten teacher, taught me that I am lovable and smart.

Aunt Hazel taught me to live life fully as an independent woman. She also taught me table manners when she took me to Clark's on Saturdays for hot chicken sandwiches with mashed potatoes and the yellow gravy I loved. And to dinner at the fancy Silver Grill in Higbee's in downtown Cleveland for the Monday evening fashion show. I did not appreciate her love of corned beef sandwiches at Max Gruber's dark noisy bar until much later in life

Woody, my stepfather, taught me integrity, honesty, and always to do my best. He also honed my sense of humor with his jokes, some raunchy, and his mischievous tricks.

Pastor Born taught me that God's love trumps church dogma, to have the courage of my convictions, and to end my sentences with a period not a question mark.

Miss Arms, my Latin teacher, taught me to do my homework every night.

Mrs. Murray, my Economics teacher, led me to Mrs. Youngjohn, a college professor, who taught me the power of words and the brain and how to teach persuasion.

Dr.Kopp, another professor, taught me that feeling special can lead to bad decisions.

Dr. Mamchur, a professor who gave blanket B's no matter the quality of the work, taught me to question authority. He was also our so-so marriage counselor before the divorce. He turned up many years later counseling my son and his wife before their wedding. Not on my advice.

Eleanor taught me friendship. How I miss our mornings over coffee cups and our shopping expeditions.

Melba, my psychotherapist, taught me to listen to my inner wisdom and trust my intuition.

Don, our leader at Haven Hill, taught me to listen and not only to words.

Doug, a counselor, taught me that secrets are corrosive.

Ginny gave me poetry.

Del taught me the power of purpose in aging.

Liz, Jer's aunt, taught me how to grow old.

Bernie, Liz's sister the nun, taught me generosity and ultimately how to die.

There are so many others, I could write a book.

Bumps and Scratches

Listen to this story:
When the soul left the body,
it was stopped by God
at heaven's gate
"You have returned just as you left:
Life is a blessing of opportunity:
Where are the bumps and scratches
left by the journey?"
Rumi

I have come to the end of these stories. I have not dwelt on the dark hours of my life and there were many. I have scars, some visible, some not, as reminders of those dark hours. But what I see now is that they were all opportunities that prepared me for better days.

I don't know anyone who has led a life without loss or turmoil, sorrow or regret . I don't know anyone who had perfect parents, perfect teachers, perfect role models. Lama Brian, a Buddhist monk, told us that our best teachers are the most annoying people in our lives. Uncomfortable as it is to deal with these folks, we should welcome them. They are mirrors of ourselves and put us in touch with our dark sides.

They teach us forgiveness. As we forgive them we deal with fewer and fewer of them. Our lives become easier. They teach us gratitude for the guides who help us on our journey. Forgiveness and gratitude ensure our happiness.

So what sense have I made of my life? What do I believe? I believe that we are all here for each other, we are all part of the grand design of the universe and we each have a part to play. The only way to understand the universe is to understand each other. The only way to understand each other is to listen to each other, to appreciate our differences, to celebrate our humanity, weaknesses and all.

In the Bourne saga, Jason is programmed to be a killing machine. But they cannot destroy his soul, his need to know the hero that he is. We are all heroes. We live in this fantastic universe where it is our task to experience as much of it as we can and find our way back to the source. We are here to learn what it is to be human. We are here to make ourselves whole. We are all part of the One. We are all made of stardust.

Acknowledgments

My special thanks to Del Jones who started the Elder Circle movement and invited me to share my story with a Wisdom Panel at Gather the Elders, an annual event in Tucson, and to the circle members who have shared their wisdom. Also to the members of Alcoholic Anonymous who have welcomed me to their meetings where I am inspired by their stories. Thank you to my poet circle, Mary Ber, Jean Dursi, and Dixie Gilbert, who have encouraged me. And to my writers workshop, Leon Alder-Bennett, John & Margaret Fleming, and Steve McGeeney, for their critical comments on clarity and grammatical matters, and especially to eagle-eyed Shirley Spitler, not only a proof reader but a friend, who turned up in my life just when I needed her. A god shot. Also for the indispensable help of Google and Goodreads.com for many of the quotations in the text and introductions to the stories.

www.ingramcontent.com/pod-product-compliance
Lightning Source LLC
Chambersburg PA
CBHW062025040426

42447CB00010B/2143